DATE DUE		

DIGGING UP
the Past

King Tut's Tomb

Essential Library

An Imprint of Abdo Publishing | www.abdopublishing.com

DIGGING UP the Past

King Tut's Tomb

BY SHANNON BAKER MOORE

CONTENT CONSULTANT
ELIZABETH MCGOVERN
EGYPTOLOGIST AND ADJUNCT LECTURER
NEW YORK UNIVERSITY

www.abdopublishing.com

Published by Abdo Publishing, a division of ABDO, PO Box 398166, Minneapolis, Minnesota 55439. Copyright © 2015 by Abdo Consulting Group, Inc. International copyrights reserved in all countries. No part of this book may be reproduced in any form without written permission from the publisher. Essential Library™ is a trademark and logo of Abdo Publishing.

Printed in the United States of America, North Mankato, Minnesota
032014
092014

THIS BOOK CONTAINS
RECYCLED MATERIALS

Cover Photo: AP Images
Interior Photos: AP Images, 2, 41; Ann Ronan Pictures/Glow Images, 6; Corbis, 10; Red Line Editorial, 12; Reed Kaestner/Corbis/Glow Images, 14; Paul Schemm/AP Images, 17; Styve Reineck/Thinkstock, 21; Thinkstock, 22; Bettmann/Corbis, 27, 37, 48; Dorling Kindersley, 31; Hulton-Deutsch Collection/Corbis, 32, 42; Stapleton Historical Collection/Glow Images, 45, 59, 62, 65, 67; Robert Harding Productions/Glow Images, 51, 55, 61; Heritage Images/Glow Images, 52, 84; SuperStock/Glow Images, 69; Werner Forman Archive/Glow Images, 72; Ann Ronan Pictures/Glow Images, 75; MIXA/Glow Images, 77; Ben Curtis/AP Images, 81, 86; Amr Nabil/AP Images, 91; Getty Images/Thinkstock, 93; Jack Fields/Corbis/Glow Images, 97

Editor: Lauren Coss
Series Designer: Becky Daum

Library of Congress Control Number: 2014932247

Cataloging-in-Publication Data

Moore, Shannon Baker.
 King Tut's tomb / Shanon Baker Moore.
  p. cm. -- (Digging up the past)
Includes bibliographical references and index.
ISBN 978-1-62403-233-2
1. Tutankhamen, King of Egypt--Tomb--Juvenile literature.   I. Title.
932/.014--dc23

2014932247

CONTENTS

The Fascinating Pharaoh

On November 26, 1922, British archaeologist Howard Carter stood in front of the door to an Egyptian tomb. For eight years, Carter had excavated in the Valley of the Kings with little to show for it. Finally, his hard work and careful research had led to the discovery of this tomb. The tomb door was sealed, plastered over, and stamped with ancient royal seals. The tomb could hold any

When Howard Carter, *left*, discovered King Tutankhamen's tomb in 1922, he renewed the world's interest in ancient Egyptian history.

THE VALLEY OF THE KINGS

In the barren hills west of the ancient Egyptian city of Thebes, there is a narrow valley known as the Valley of the Kings. Most of the pharaohs from the New Kingdom, which lasted from the 1500s to 1000s BCE, are buried in this valley. During the ancient Egyptian periods called the Old and Middle Kingdoms, which last from the 2500s to the 1600s BCE, pharaohs were buried in pyramids. Pyramids were impressive burial monuments for the kings, but tomb robbers knew incredible riches were buried with the pharaohs. Tomb robbers looted the pyramids and destroyed the bodies. Eventually, pharaohs started building secret tombs in the desolate Valley of the Kings. More than 60 tombs have been discovered in this valley.

number of treasures and artifacts. It might even be the burial place of a pharaoh, an ancient Egyptian king.

Ancient Egyptians believed in an afterlife. According to ancient Egyptian belief, the afterlife was similar to the living world, only better. Egyptians buried their dead with the supplies they would need for the next life. Tombs, such as the one Carter discovered, should contain everything a person might need in the next life. Pharaohs were buried with all kinds of treasures, including jewelry, furniture, expensive clothing, and even food and wine.

Such valuable treasures appealed to modern-day explorers and ancient tomb robbers alike. As Carter examined the tomb, he could tell it had been robbed. He saw evidence of two break-ins. However, the tomb's seals remained intact, meaning Egyptian officials had inspected and resealed the tomb in ancient times. It was likely the tomb had lain undisturbed for thousands of years.

Carter poked a small hole into the upper left corner of the doorway. He lit a candle and stuck it into the hole. He peered into the first room of the tomb. According to Carter, "Details of the room within emerged slowly from the mist, strange animals, statues, and gold—everywhere the glint of gold."[1]

Lord Carnarvon, the man who had funded the excavation, stood next to Carter. "Can you see anything?" Carnarvon asked eagerly.[2]

Stunned at the treasures before him, Carter could barely reply.

"Yes," he said, "wonderful things."[3]

THE IMPACT OF TUT'S TOMB

Carter had discovered the tomb of the Egyptian pharaoh Tutankhamen, soon nicknamed "King Tut." The find astonished the world. Tutankhamen's tomb was one of the most important archaeological discoveries in history, and it was one of the greatest royal treasures ever found. Before the stunning

HOWARD CARTER

Carter was born in London, Great Britain, on May 9, 1874. He arrived in Egypt in October 1891, when he was 17 years old. While working as an artist and draftsman, Carter also learned how to excavate. From 1899 to 1905, Carter worked as inspector of the Valley of the Kings for Upper Egypt. As inspector, Carter had many responsibilities, including supervising digs, restoring sites, installing electric lights in tombs, and building metal gates to protect tombs. After losing his job due to a dispute with some tourists, Carter managed to scrape out a meager living selling paintings to tourists and dealing in antiquities until 1907, when Lord Carnarvon hired him.

Carter had a reputation for being gruff, unpolished, and at times even rude. Nevertheless, he was a thorough and careful archaeologist. After his ten-year excavation of Tut's tomb, Carter returned to London, where he lived until his death on March 2, 1939.

Carter devoted much of his life to finding and studying Tut's tomb.

discovery of King Tut's tomb, public interest in archaeology was declining. The tomb, full of treasures, reawakened interest in archaeology and ancient Egyptian civilization. King Tut's mummy, which had been undisturbed for thousands of years, also helped researchers identify other unknown mummies.

EGYPTMANIA

Throughout history, people have been fascinated by ancient Egyptian culture. From the Roman Empire to modern times, Egyptian religion, art, and architecture have influenced and inspired people. Interest was especially high following the discovery of Tutankhamen's tomb in 1922. Bright primary colors, rich materials, and exotic feathers—as had been found in Egyptian tombs—became popular. A good example of Egyptmania was the Astoria movie theatre in Great Britain. The lobby had lotus-blossom pillars, bright red walls, and designs of green, gold, and black. Its women's restroom displayed a wall mural of an Egyptian woman bathing in a lotus-filled pool. The theatre auditorium was also decorated in red, gold, and black with a mural depicting scenes from ancient Egyptian history.

In Carter's day, people were fascinated by the boy-king Tutankhamen and his spectacular tomb. The *Times*, a London newspaper, described the tomb as "the most sensational Egyptological discovery of the century."[4] People traveled from all around the world to see the tomb.

WHERE IS KING TUT'S TOMB?

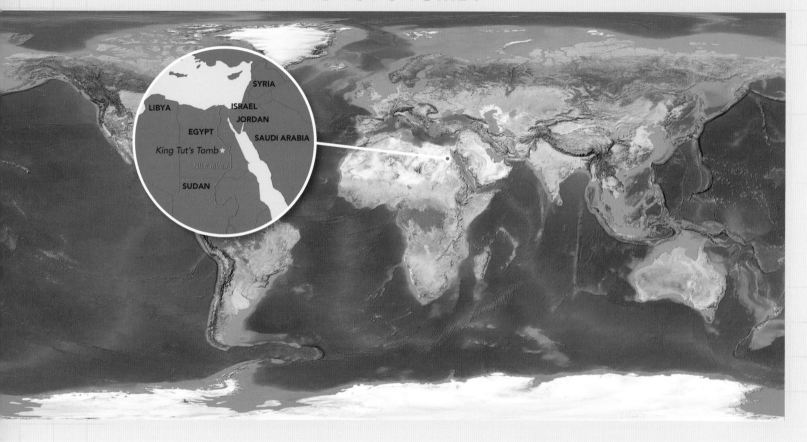

SYRIA
LIBYA
ISRAEL
JORDAN
EGYPT
SAUDI ARABIA
King Tut's Tomb
NILE RIVER
SUDAN

Newspapers competed against one another to publish the most sensational story about the discovery, but most of the stories held little truth. Some said Tut's mummy was cursed. Rumors spread about how the curse of the mummy was killing people. Hollywood made mummy movies. Egyptmania and Tutmania spread, as jewelry, clothing, furniture, and even buildings were designed to reflect ancient Egyptian artistic styles.

Interest in Egypt and King Tut continued through the 1900s. In the early 2000s, King Tut and his treasures traveled to museums worldwide, and the King Tut exhibit has attracted millions of visitors. Documentaries and television shows continue to be made about Tutankhamen. Many scholars and researchers have studied King Tut's blood type, DNA, and computed tomography (CT) scans, comparing them to other mummies. Archaeologists still search for clues about his life and reign. Tourists still travel to Egypt to visit Tutankhamen's tomb.

The Pharaoh Tutankhamen was a boy who became king more than 3,000 years ago. Researchers believe he was only eight or nine years old when he took the throne. He ruled for ten years, from 1333 to 1323 BCE. Nevertheless, Tut may be the most famous king in the world.

2

Tutankhamen's Life and Reign

The Egyptian king Tutankhamen is such a famous pharaoh today few people realize he almost disappeared from history. In fact, very little is known about his life. Much of Egyptology is a matter of debate. Like detectives, scholars and experts search for evidence. Then they form conclusions based on their interpretations of the evidence. Egyptologists and other experts disagree about rulers, dates, and events. People's opinions change as they make new discoveries. More than 3,000 years have passed

A golden throne with a carving depicting Tutankhamen and his wife was found in the king's tomb.

since Tutankhamen ruled Egypt, and much of what is known about him is based on educated guesswork.

Tutankhamen became pharaoh when he was only eight or nine years old. His ten-year reign ended with his death at approximately age 18 or 19. Tutankhamen was pharaoh during the period of Egyptian history known as the New Kingdom. During the New Kingdom, there were three powerful periods—the Eighteenth Dynasty, the Nineteenth Dynasty, and the Twentieth Dynasty. Tutankhamen's reign occurred during the Eighteenth Dynasty.

BEFORE TUTANKHAMEN

Tutankhamen's father, Akhenaton, was a very controversial pharaoh. Known as the heretic king, Akhenaton dramatically changed the religious and political traditions of Egypt. Many of these traditions had been in place for centuries. Akhenaton refused to worship the many Egyptian gods, particularly the chief god at the time, Amon. Instead he worshiped only one god, the sun disk known as the Aton. He built a new capital city at Amarna, approximately 200 miles (322 km) south of modern Cairo. He refused to leave Amarna to take part in the traditional duties of a pharaoh, such as going to battle or traveling Egypt to visit his people. Akhenaton's reign later became known as the Amarna Period.

TUTANKHAMEN'S REIGN—A RETURN TO TRADITION

Most scholars believe Tutankhamen was born in Amarna in approximately 1341 BCE and was originally named *Tutankhaten*, a name that means "living image of Aton." After his father's death in approximately 1335 BCE, Tutankhaten became king. The royal court moved from Amarna back to Thebes. Since he was only a child when he became king, Tutankhaten had advisers to help him rule. Tutankhaten changed his name to *Tutankhamen*, the "living image of Amon" to show he was returning

A stela, or inscribed stone slab, shows Akhenaton worshiping the sun god.

MANY GODS

Religion was an important part of daily life in Egypt. Ancient Egyptians were polytheistic, which means they worshiped many gods. There were many Egyptian gods and goddesses, and they were shown in many different forms. Amon, the king of the gods, could appear as a ram, a ram-headed man, a frog-headed man, a goose, or a man wearing a tall, double-plumed headdress.

the country to its traditional ways. Tutankhamen married his half sister, Ankhesenpaaton, later known as Ankhesenamen. At the time, it was common for royalty to marry within their families to help preserve the royal line.

Tutankhamen tried to separate his rule from the disastrous reign of his father. Similar to other Egyptian rulers, Tut built massive monuments and temples to honor Egyptian gods. In many of his building projects, the young king emphasized his connection to the god Amon and traditional Egyptian ways.

Tut's attempts to separate himself from his father were mostly unsuccessful, however. After Tut's death in 1323 BCE, his reign was deliberately deleted from history. In ancient Egypt, it was not unusual for new rulers to erase a previous pharaoh's name or image on monuments and to insert their own name or image instead. Tut's name was removed from monuments after his death. But the pharaohs after King Tut took this deletion one step further. Amarna was also demolished, and its stones were used for other building projects. The official list of Eighteenth Dynasty kings excluded the names of all the pharaohs associated with the Amarna Period, including Tutankhamen's. It was as if roughly 30 years of history had never happened. Nevertheless, traces of Tutankhamen remained, waiting to be discovered by the detectives of ancient history—archaeologists.

EXPLORING ANCIENT EGYPT

People were interested in Egyptian history long before Howard Carter first stood before Tut's tomb in the 1920s. In 1798, French leader Napoléon Bonaparte led a military expedition to Egypt. He brought along 167 scholars who were tasked with studying the country's culture, geography, and ancient history.

These scholars worked in Egypt for three years. In 1799, Napoléon's scholars discovered the Rosetta Stone. With this stone, which is inscribed in three languages, scholars were eventually able to decipher ancient Egyptian hieroglyphs. Hieroglyphs are the distinctive picture writing that appears on the tombs, monuments, papyrus, and art of ancient Egypt. But no scholars in Napoléon's time were able to read them. The Rosetta Stone features the same inscription written in three languages: ancient Egyptian hieroglyphs, Demotic, and Greek. In 1822, Jean-François Champollion published a key to translating hieroglyphs. For the first time since ancient times, scholars could actually read the inscriptions on ancient Egyptian artifacts.

FINDING TUT'S NAME

In 1891, British archaeologist William Matthew Flinders Petrie began excavating at Amarna, Tutankhamen's boyhood home. Petrie wanted to learn about ancient Egyptian life so he could study and preserve the past. Petrie's diggers sifted through the royal trash heaps. Petrie realized the things people throw away reveal much about their daily lives.

In the royal trash, Petrie discovered objects with Tutankhamen's name on them. Monuments and inscriptions in other locations had also confirmed the existence of the mysterious King Tutankhamen, but very little was known about him. At Amarna, Petrie found dozens of bright blue finger rings

DECIPHERING HIEROGLYPHICS

The Egyptians left out vowels from their hieroglyphic texts, just as people often do today when they send text messages. Because ancient Egyptian is no longer spoken, Egyptologists must guess which vowels ancient Egyptians might have used. Usually Egyptologists use e. However, no one is certain which vowels ancient Egyptian writers used or where they placed them in a word. As a result, most ancient Egyptian names have many different spelling variations in English. For example, King Tut's name can be spelled in several ways. *Tutankhamen*, *Tutankhamun*, and *Tutankhamon* are the most common, but *Touatankhamanou*, *Tut.ankh. Amen*, and *Tutenchamun* have also been used.

Ancient Egyptians used a pictorial writing system known as hieroglyphs. Each symbol represented an object or a sound or group of sounds.

made from a ceramic called faience. In hieroglyphic writing, royal names are written inside an oval outline known as a cartouche. Many of the rings Petrie found were inscribed with Tut's cartouche. Petrie's finds confirmed the existence of this unknown king, and the finger rings suggested Tut was connected with Amarna. The previously unknown King Tut was now identified as a member of the royal family at Amarna.

Other Tut artifacts were also found elsewhere in Egypt. A few figures of Tutankhamen were found at temples and palaces. Fragments of a box, a jar, and other rings included Tutankhamen's name. But where was Tut's mummy?

3

Clues to Tutankhamen

In the early 1900s, excavating Egyptian tombs was costly and time-consuming. Wealthy individuals interested in Egyptology funded many digs. These wealthy patrons then hired archaeology experts to run and manage the excavations.

In the early 1900s, many archaeologists scoured Egypt's Valley of the Kings, searching for ancient tombs and the treasure they might contain.

EXCAVATING IN EGYPT

In order to excavate, archaeologists needed a concession from the Egyptian Antiquities Service. A concession granted permission to excavate, stating where an archaeologist could dig and for how long. No one could dig on another person's concession, and any archaeological finds were usually split between the Antiquities Service and the excavator.

Wealthy American lawyer and businessman Theodore Davis funded several excavations in Egypt in the early 1900s. From 1902 to 1914, Davis had a concession in the Valley of the Kings. Excavators before Davis had said there was nothing left to find in the Valley. But Davis believed they were wrong. At the time, Carter was working as inspector of the Valley of the Kings. As a second job, Carter helped supervise Davis's excavation. In 1904, however, Carter was transferred to Saqqara, a different area of Egypt. He could no longer work for Davis.

THREE CLUES

Despite widespread tomb robbing, the valley yielded new finds. During his excavations in the Valley of the Kings, Davis found three items connected to Tutankhamen. During the excavation of 1905–1906, Davis's chief archaeologist, Edward Ayrton, found a ceramic cup inscribed with Tut's name wedged under a rock.

In 1907, Davis and his crew discovered a second clue to Tutankhamen's existence—a small pit containing large white jars. Inside the jars were seals with Tutankhamen's name; bundles of natron, a substance used to mummify bodies; collars made of real flowers, which were worn at funerals; a miniature mummy mask; and the remains of a meal.

Davis's team found a third Tutankhamen-related object in 1909. They discovered a small, unfinished chamber that held figurines and some gold foil bearing Tutankhamen's name. Davis mistakenly believed this small chamber was the long-lost tomb of Pharaoh Tutankhamen. He published a book about his find, and in that book he stated, "I fear the Valley is now exhausted."[1]

Carter thought Davis was wrong, and he wanted to search for Tutankhamen. In 1907, he got his lucky break. He was recommended as an excavator to wealthy Englishman Lord Carnarvon.

CARTER JOINS CARNARVON

George Edward Stanhope Molyneux Herbert, fifth Earl of Carnarvon, was a wealthy British aristocrat. Lord Carnarvon, as he was called, had originally come to Egypt in 1903. Once there, he had become interested in Egyptology. Initially, Carnarvon did not have much success, although he did manage to dig up a mummified cat. He was an enthusiastic amateur who knew he needed help from someone with greater expertise. His search for an experienced archaeologist led him to Carter. Carnarvon offered Carter a job, and Carter eagerly agreed. Carnarvon would provide the money to excavate; Carter would provide the know-how.

From the start, Carter and Carnarvon wanted to dig in the Valley of the Kings, but they were unable to because the concession still belonged to Davis. Carnarvon had a concession that allowed him to excavate at Thebes. From 1907 to 1912, Carter and Carnarvon excavated near Thebes. They then moved northward, but the conditions of the Nile delta made excavation more difficult. They were forced to abandon one site because it was infested with poisonous snakes.

Finally, in 1914, Davis decided to give up his concession in the Valley of the Kings. He believed he had found the destroyed tomb of Tutankhamen, and there was nothing left to find. In reality, he had not discovered the tomb,

LORD CARNARVON

George Edward Stanhope Molyneux Herbert, fifth Earl of Carnarvon, was the wealthy British aristocrat who funded Carter's excavations. Born on June 26, 1866, Carnarvon lived on his family's estate, Highclere Castle. He was an avid sportsman and art collector. In 1903, Carnarvon came to Egypt to recuperate from an automobile accident. There he developed an interest in Egyptology. Carnarvon and Carter worked together from 1907 until Carnarvon's death on April 5, 1923. He died at age 57 from an infected mosquito bite.

Lord Carnarvon, shortly before his death in 1923

although he had come extremely close. Harry Burton, an expert who worked for Davis at the time later said,

> If Mr. Theodore Davis . . . had not stopped his last "dig" too soon I am convinced he would have discovered the present tomb of King Tutankhamen. We came within six feet of it.[2]

CARNARVON'S CONCESSION

As soon as Davis gave up the concession to the Valley of the Kings, Carnarvon immediately applied for it. In June 1914, after seven years of waiting, Carter and Carnarvon received the concession. Finally they could search for the long lost tomb of Tutankhamen. They began preparing for what Carter called "a systematic and exhaustive search" for Tut.[3] The cup, the gold foil, and the remains of the meal had convinced Carter Tutankhamen's tomb remained to be found. In addition, nearby tombs held remains from Amarna royalty, who may have been Tutankhamen's relatives. As Carter said,

> With all this evidence before us, we were thoroughly convinced in our own minds that the tomb of Tut-ankh-Amen was still to find, and that it ought to be situated not far from the centre of The Valley.[4]

But Carter and Carnarvon would have to wait to discover what secrets the Valley of the Kings still held. In 1914, World War I (1914–1918) broke out, and once again Carter and Carnarvon were unable to dig in the valley.

Carnarvon was stuck in Great Britain because of the dangers of travel, while Carter, who spoke fluent Arabic, worked with the British Intelligence Department in Cairo. In 1917, as the war drew to a close, Carter and Carnarvon were able to officially begin their search for Tutankhamen's tomb.

CARTER THE ARTIST

In addition to being a skilled archaeologist, Carter was also a talented artist. He had grown up in a family of artists, and his father enjoyed a successful career as a painter and illustrator. When he first came to Egypt, Carter used his talent to help with tracings of tomb scenes, sometimes drawing from seven o'clock in the morning until sunset. Carter used his artistic talent throughout his career. When he was temporarily unemployed, he supported himself by painting watercolor pictures for tourists and creating illustrations for Egyptology books. During the excavation of Tut's tomb, Carter drew scale drawings that provided valuable details that otherwise may have been lost.

DIGGING DEEPER

How to Make a Mummy

Egyptians made mummies to preserve the human body after death. The mummification process took 70 days. First, embalmers washed the body in natron solution. This saltlike substance helped preserve and disinfect the body. Then the embalmers removed the brain by inserting a thin hook up the nose. They rotated the hook, which broke the brain into pieces. Then they turned the body over, and the pieces of brain ran out through the nose. After cleaning out the skull, the embalmers poured in resin. Next, they cut a slit on the left side of the body and removed four internal organs—the liver, lungs, intestines, and stomach. The heart was left in the body. The internal organs were preserved and placed in four canopic jars. The corpse was packed inside and out with natron to dehydrate it.

After 40 days, the embalmers removed the natron, washed and oiled the body, then packed it with linen and resin.

Wrapping the mummy took 15 days. Fingers and toes were each wrapped separately before the rest of the body. Bandages, linen pads, and sheets were used as needed to give the mummy a more human shape. If a body part was missing, an artificial body part would be wrapped in its place.

Ancient Egyptians believed mummification would help preserve a body for the afterlife.

4

Finding the Tomb

According to Carter,

> The difficulty [in finding Tutankhamen's tomb] was to know where to begin, for mountains of rubbish thrown out by previous excavators encumbered the ground in all directions, and no sort of record had ever been kept as to which areas had been properly excavated and which had not.[1]

It would take five years of backbreaking excavation for Carter and his workers to finally find and uncover Tut's tomb.

THE HUNT FOR ROYAL TOMBS

Pharaohs ruled ancient Egypt for thousands of years, but in early excavations of ancient Egypt, no mummy of a pharaoh had ever been found. Then in 1881, officials located a tomb full of royal mummies—400 years' worth of mummies. Egyptologists determined these mummies had been moved from their original tombs to protect them from thieves. This cache of mummies became known as the Dayr al-Bahrī Cache, after the location in which it was found. In 1898, another cache was discovered. These royal caches suggested the mummies of many pharaohs had not yet been found.

Carter felt there was only one way to ensure that nothing was overlooked. He needed to systemically dig all the way down to the bedrock.

THE HUNT BEGINS

Carter made a detailed map of the Valley of the Kings. He marked every area previously excavated and the exact spot where each excavated object had been found. His research convinced him there were areas in the valley that had been missed because they were covered by debris from previous digs. Based on his investigation, Carter decided the most likely location for Tutankhamen's tomb was in a triangle-shaped area between three other royal tombs.

Digging down to bedrock required removing thousands and thousands of tons of limestone debris. Underneath the rubble of previous digs was a hard layer of sediment created by previous flooding. The Valley of the Kings is a wadi, or dry riverbed, that lies between white limestone cliffs. The desert landscape rarely gets any rain. However, severe thunderstorms, which occasionally strike the valley, can cause flash floods, sweeping stones, sand, and debris down the dry riverbed.

Near the end of the Eighteenth Dynasty, a flash flood deposited a layer of sediment, mud, chalk, shale, and limestone on top of Tut's tomb. The tomb was completely buried and hidden from further break-ins. In fact, the tomb was so well hidden that almost 200 years later, in approximately 1143 BCE, builders working on the tomb of Pharaoh Ramses VI did not even know Tut's tomb existed. They built stone huts directly on top of the site and quarried Ramses VI's tomb entrance directly above Tut's tomb. In doing so, the workers unintentionally helped hide and protect Tut's tomb from future thieves.

"In a few moments the whole mountain-side foamed with innumerable cascades. The tomb in the cleft was filled to its brim with rainwater, and we had but a few minutes to strike camp for higher ground, clear of the boulder-strewn valley which soon became a roaring torrent."[2]

—HOWARD CARTER, DESCRIBING THE FURY OF A FLASH FLOOD IN 1916

BACKBREAKING WORK

In the fall of 1917, hundreds of workers, both men and boys, began the backbreaking work of excavation. To avoid the worst of the desert heat,

CARTER AND THE EGYPTIANS

Since the 1500s, Egypt was dominated by stronger European nations. It became a British protectorate in 1914 during World War I. In 1922, Egypt gained its independence. Carter lived in an era when European nations had colonized countries around the globe. Many Europeans had little respect for the native peoples of the countries they ruled. Carter, on the other hand, was usually respectful of Egyptians and their culture. He got along well with Egyptians. He learned to speak Arabic, and he considered Egypt his home. In the preface to his book about Tut's tomb, Carter thanked the Egyptian workmen "who have loyally and conscientiously carried out every duty which I entrusted to them."[3]

the digging season in Egypt occurred in fall and winter, but even then the weather could get as hot as 95 degrees Fahrenheit (35°C). Sweating under the hot Egyptian sun, workers thoroughly inspected each basket of limestone rubble before it was hauled off and dumped. Carter worked methodically and carefully. He may have been looking for the buried treasure of a king, but he would never knowingly ignore or toss out other possible artifacts of archaeological interest, such as bits of metal, broken glass, pottery shards, or beads.

Egyptian laborers performed much of the backbreaking excavation work.

Carter's workers chipped away at the hard ground, heaped rubble into baskets, hoisted the heavy baskets onto their shoulders, and then hauled away the debris. A hand-propelled railway was also installed to help move debris. Carter and his team cleared away the upper layers of the dig site until they reached the base of the tomb of Ramses VI and the workmen's huts. They wanted to clear this area, too. But Ramses VI's tomb was a popular tourist attraction. If Carter continued digging, he would block tourist access to the Ramses VI tomb. He and Carnarvon decided to stop and dig in a more convenient place. The two men had no idea how close they were to Tut's tomb. Only a few feet more, and they would have found it.

Instead, Carter and Carnarvon dug in other locations in the Valley of the Kings. They found ostraca, limestone flakes used by ancient quarry teams to jot down notes, similar to scratch paper. They found 13 beautiful alabaster jars.[4] But they found no tomb. According to Carter, "We had now dug in The Valley for several seasons with extremely scanty results."[5] The two men had excavated for five expensive years with little success. Carnarvon was spending a fortune, and he was ready to quit.

In the summer of 1922, Carter received an invitation to Carnarvon's home at Highclere Castle. Carnarvon reviewed their work together and thanked Carter. Then he broke the bad news: Carnarvon was going to end the excavation. Carter showed Carnarvon a map that marked every place they had excavated. There was one place left, the ground under the workmen's huts near the tomb of Ramses VI. Carter asked Carnarvon for one more season. "So long as a single area of untouched ground remained," said

Carter, "the risk was worth taking."[7] Carnarvon relented. Carter could have one more season.

CARTER'S LAST CHANCE

November 1922 began just like every other season with one critical difference—everyone at the dig knew this season would be their last. If they did not find Tutankhamen's tomb now, they never would. On November 1, 1922, Carter's workmen were ready to begin. They focused their efforts on the ground beneath the ancient stone huts. Built approximately three feet (0.9 m) above bedrock, the huts dated from the Twentieth Dynasty (1196–1070 BCE). Laborers working on the nearby tomb of Ramses VI had most

THE INFLUENCE OF PETRIE

Carter's excavation methods were influenced by archaeologist William Matthew Flinders Petrie, who had found evidence of Tut's existence while excavating at Amarna. Petrie pushed for more scientific methods and protested against careless techniques, which often destroyed valuable historical evidence. Petrie dug more than 50 sites throughout Egypt and the Middle East. He wrote more than 100 books and 1,000 articles. Carter met Petrie shortly after arriving in Egypt. Carter later said of the archaeologist, "Petrie's training during those months transformed me, I believe, into something of the nature of an investigator, [teaching me] to dig and examine systematically."[8]

likely used the huts. By the evening of November 3, Carter's men had moved the stone huts out of the way. On November 4, they began clearing away the dirt above the bedrock.

The dig was usually a noisy place, full of the clang of pickaxes and shovels, the clatter of stones and rubble, and the grunts and shouts of workmen. So when everything suddenly went silent, Carter knew something unusual had happened. The diggers had discovered a step underneath the very first hut they had checked. It seemed almost too good to be true. Could Carter have found the tomb?

A bit more digging revealed a sunken stairway. This was the discovery Carter had longed for. Still, he did not yet know if this truly was the tomb of Tutankhamen. Carter's team dug feverishly the rest of the day and into the next. On the afternoon of November 5, they finally cleared away enough rubble to see all four sides of the descending stairwell.

They cleared away step after step, revealing a passageway ten feet (3 m) high and six feet (1.8 m) wide.[9] By dusk, the diggers had cleared away 12 steps. The upper part of a doorway, which was plastered and sealed shut, was visible. Carter could not see the entire door—that would require more digging—but he carefully examined the intact seals that were visible. The upper part of the door was stamped with ancient royal seals showing a jackal crouching above nine bound captives. The nine bound captives represented the nine traditional enemies of Egypt. The jackal was the guardian of royal cemeteries. This was the distinctive seal of the royal necropolis, the ancient royal cemetery. These intact necropolis seals proved someone of noble birth was buried in the tomb. Since the huts had been built directly on top of it, Carter knew the tomb had not been disturbed since at least the Twentieth Dynasty or before, almost 3,000 years earlier.

The discovery of the entrance to King Tutankhamen's tomb was the breakthrough Carter had been waiting for.

5

Opening the Tomb

As Carter examined the seals on the tomb door, he noticed a spot where some plaster had fallen off. He made a small hole, big enough to insert a flashlight, and peered in. The passage on the other side of the door was packed with stones and rubble from the floor to the ceiling. This barrier further blocked the tomb's entrance and provided additional protection for the tomb.

With the tomb entrance finally discovered, exploration of King Tutankhamen's tomb could begin.

Carter was thrilled. "Anything, literally anything might lie beyond that passage," he said, "and it needed all my self-control to keep from breaking down the doorway, and investigating then and there."[1] One thing confused him, however. Why was the tomb opening so small? Most royal tombs in the Valley of the Kings were much larger. Typically royal tombs were massive structures with intricate wall paintings. Pharaohs started construction on their tombs as soon as they were crowned, and royal tombs took years to complete. The small size of this tomb seemed to indicate it was a cache for mummies or the tomb of a nobleman. It seemed unlikely such a small tomb belonged to a pharaoh.

> "At last have made wonderful discovery in Valley; a magnificent tomb with seals intact; recovered same for your arrival; congratulations."[2]
>
> —CARTER'S TELEGRAM TO CARNARVON ON THE MORNING AFTER CARTER UNCOVERED TUT'S TOMB

THE WAIT

Carter was eager to open the tomb, but Lord Carnarvon was in Great Britain. Carter felt it was only fair to wait for Carnarvon's arrival before opening the tomb. On November 6, Carter sent a telegram to Carnarvon and then anxiously awaited his arrival. To protect the tomb, Carter had his workers refill the excavation site. They poured stones and rubble back into the stairwell,

Carter, *right*, waited until Lord Carnarvon, *left*, and his daughter, Evelyn, *center*, arrived to officially open and explore the tomb.

filling it up to ground level. They rolled back the large boulders that had covered the site. It was impossible to tell a tomb had ever been there. Carter said it was as if "the tomb had vanished."[3]

After three long weeks, Carnarvon finally arrived, and on November 24, he and Carter were back at the tomb. Carter's friend, Arthur Callender, a retired engineer and architect, and Carnarvon's daughter, Lady Evelyn Herbert, joined them.

TWO TOMB DOORS

Carter and Carnarvon examined the tomb door once again. The doorway and all 16 steps leading down to it had been completely excavated before Carnarvon's arrival. They could now see additional seals. In addition to the necropolis seals Carter had examined earlier, they discovered seals bearing Tutankhamen's name.

While excavating the stairwell, Carter had found potsherds, or pottery fragments, and boxes with the names of many different pharaohs mixed with the rubble. Carter also determined the tomb had been broken into more than once. The tomb had been sealed after Tut's

BRACING FOR DISAPPOINTMENT

Carter had good reason to worry his excavation would end in disappointment. In 1900, he had found the entrance to a tomb at Dayr al-Bahrī. Inside was a six-foot- (1.8 m) tall statue and some other artifacts.[4] His hopes rose as he anticipated finding an intact tomb. But further excavation revealed a small chamber "full of rubbish" and a few insignificant artifacts.[5] Carter's disappointment at Dayr al-Bahrī made him question his 1922 discovery. Compared to other royal tombs in the Valley of the Kings, Tutankhamen's tomb is quite small. The tomb seemed more suited for nobility or as a mummy cache. The debris in the stairwell and tunnel seemed to confirm Carter had found a cache because artifacts from several different pharaohs were buried in the rubble.

burial and then resealed later, after it had been robbed. This meant the tomb was only partially intact. Carter assumed the tomb still held something valuable, because it made no sense to reseal an empty tomb. But he worried that, as with some other tombs he had found, the tomb held next to nothing. There was no way to be sure until the tomb was opened.

ROBBING TUTANKHAMEN'S TOMB

Carter concluded Tutankhamen's tomb had been robbed a few years after his burial. Carter also determined the tomb was robbed at least twice. Carter thought robbers broke in through the upper left corner of the first sealed door and made a hole just large enough for a man. They then tunneled through to the second door, carved a hole through the second door, and started looting. Carter saw evidence that objects had been scattered and then hastily repacked. He also found objects with pieces in multiple boxes as well as strewn across the floor. Based on what he saw, Carter speculated the robbers had difficultly seeing. In their rush to rob the tomb, they picked up items, thinking they were solid gold, then tossed them aside when they realized the items were only gilded wood.

The next day, on November 25, Carter and Carnarvon opened the tomb and removed the sealed door. There lay the passageway, packed floor to ceiling with rubble. The rubble showed signs of robbery. The sloping passageway was six feet (1.8 m) wide and almost seven feet (2.1 m) high, and it was packed with two kinds of debris.[6] Most of the rubble was white limestone chips, but a line of dark flint chips filled the upper-left corner of the passageway. This indicated that a tunnel had been dug through the limestone at one point. Carter figured tomb robbers had tunneled into the tomb, but cemetery officials had discovered the tunnel and blocked it to prevent further looting.

As they cleared the passageway, they found artifacts mixed in with the rubble, including broken pots, water skins, alabaster jars, vases, and fragments of other objects. The broken artifacts offered more evidence of plundering. Carter made sure the workmen meticulously removed the debris.

Egyptian laborers removed vast amounts of debris and damaged artifacts from the tomb.

Carnarvon estimated they moved between 150,000 and 200,000 short tons (136,000 and 181,000 metric tons) of debris.[7] Finally, in the middle of the afternoon of November 26, they found a second sealed doorway. Carter said, "[This] was the day of days, the most wonderful that I have ever lived through, and certainly one whose like I can never hope to see again."[8]

They were 30 feet (9.1 m) from the outer door, and this second doorway was almost identical to the first. Like the first doorway, it bore seals of both the necropolis and Tutankhamen. It also showed signs of having been opened and then resealed. Carter and Carnarvon were convinced they had discovered a cache, not a tomb.

THE FIRST GLIMPSE

The debris was finally cleared. After weeks of waiting, it was time to open the tomb. Carter's hands trembled as he carved a tiny hole in the upper-left corner and inserted a metal rod. He gently poked and prodded. Nothing. Empty space lay behind the door.

NUMBERING TOMBS

The Valley of the Kings contains tombs from many time periods. In 1827, Egyptologist John Gardner Wilkinson surveyed the 21 known tombs in the valley. He numbered each tomb as he came to it, and his numbering system became the standard for numbering tombs in the Valley of the Kings. Tombs are numbered chronologically in the order they are found. Tutankhamen's tomb is KV (King's Valley) 62. The next tomb, KV63, was not discovered until March 10, 2005. Other abbreviations used for tombs are WV for Western Valley, QV for Queen's Valley, DB for Dayr al-Baḥrī, and TT for Thebes.

Carter lit a candle to test for harmful gases that might be lingering in the tomb. Then he widened the hole and peered in:

> At first I could see nothing, the hot air escaping from the chamber causing the candle flame to flicker, but presently, as my eyes grew accustomed to the light, details of the room within emerged slowly from the mist, strange animals, statues, and gold—everywhere the glint of gold. For the moment—an eternity it must have seemed to the others standing by—I was struck dumb with amazement, and when Lord Carnarvon, unable to stand the suspense any longer, inquired anxiously, "Can you see anything?" It was all I could do to get out the words, "Yes, wonderful things."[9]

Carter enlarged the hole so they could both see in, and by flashlight they explored the vast archaeological fortune spread before them—the treasures of Pharaoh Tutankhamen.

A statue of the god Anubis was one of the many artifacts discovered in Tutankhamen's tomb.

6

Inside the Tomb

The second tomb door was officially opened on November 27, 1922. Carter had electric lights installed, and he and Carnarvon now fully examined the organized chaos of the tomb. Eventually, they learned, the tomb had four rooms: the Antechamber, the Burial Chamber, the Annex, and the Treasury.

The four rooms of Tut's tomb, including the Antechamber, were full of valuable treasure and historic artifacts.

PRECIOUS OBJECTS

The tomb held thousands of valuable objects that were thousands of years old and incredibly fragile. The Antechamber alone held between 600 and 700 items.[1] In the Antechamber, across from the entrance, were three large golden couches carved in the shapes of animals, including a lion, a cow, and a crocodile. Tut's mummy would have been placed on each couch during the various stages of embalming. Piled on top of the couches and packed underneath were dozens of other objects—chairs, a throne, vases, shrines, white oval boxes, staves, beds, a figure of the king, chests and

PREPARING FOR THE AFTERLIFE

Ancient Egyptians were buried with possessions they would need in the next life. A pharaoh would need jewelry, makeup, perfume, shoes, clothing, thrones, chariots, food, wine, fans, beds, and much more. Tutankhamen took three sets of board games with him to the afterlife.[2] Thirty-six jars of wine would quench his thirst.[3] He would also want special mementos from his past life, such as the lock of hair from his grandmother, Queen Tiy, which was found in the Treasury. Tut had items from his childhood, including a child-sized throne, clothes, and child-sized weapons. Ancient Egyptians also took *shabtis* with them to the next world. According to Egyptian tradition, these small statues could come to life and do the deceased's bidding. For example, if the gods in the next world needed the deceased to work in the fields, the deceased would send the *shabtis*. Tut's tomb contained 413 *shabtis*.[4]

The Wishing Cup found in Tutankhamen's tomb is made of the mineral calcite.

boxes, and floral and leaf bouquets. To the left of the doorway was a jumble of chariot pieces. To the right were two life-size statues of the king, facing each other and appearing to guard a sealed doorway. On the floor near the Antechamber entrance sat a beautiful translucent cup in the shape of a lotus flower, which Carter and Carnarvon called the Wishing Cup.

Between the two king statues was another sealed doorway. A small, resealed hole near the bottom suggested the room beyond had been broken into by robbers and resealed. Carter, Carnarvon, and Lady Evelyn reopened this small hole. Carter was a meticulous excavator, and normally he never would have taken such a liberty. But in 1900, Carter had found another sealed tomb which, when opened, contained only a statue, an empty coffin, and a few funerary offerings. Carter had announced the discovery and invited officials to the opening, only to suffer bitter disappointment and embarrassment. He did not want that to happen again. This time Carter examined the contents ahead of time. He wiggled in the hole and saw the huge gold shrines of the Burial Chamber and the Treasury room beyond. After Carter, Carnarvon, and Lady Evelyn checked the contents, Carter resealed the hole and covered the newly plastered area with a basket and some reeds. The Burial Chamber would not be officially opened and inspected until after the Antechamber was cleared.

Underneath one of the couches in the Antechamber was a small opening that led into another sealed doorway. This was the doorway to the Annex, a room smaller than the Antechamber but

TUTANKHAMEN'S WEAPONS

Tutankhamen was buried with many of his weapons. Bows, arrows, boomerangs, clubs, daggers, swords, batons, slings, and throwing-sticks were all found in his tomb. Along with 30 bows, the tomb held a bow box and 295 arrows.[5] Some of the bows were child-sized, and there was a child-sized sword as well. Carter also found armor, including a leather chest plate and eight shields, in the tomb.[6] Some shields were clearly ceremonial because of their elaborate decoration. Tutankhamen also had two daggers bound in his mummy wrappings.

even more crowded and disorganized. It looked as if robbers had raided the room and then left everything in a heap after they had stolen what they could. The entire floor was covered with objects.

IN THE CARE OF EXPERTS

The sheer number of objects was overwhelming. It would take tremendous care to record, move, and preserve each object. Carter realized the difficulty of his task and quickly assembled a team of specialists. The team included a photographer, a chemist, two Egyptologists, two draftsmen, a historian, a hieroglyph expert, and an architect with engineering experience.

The tomb objects were so fragile they could disintegrate as soon they were touched or moved. For example, Carter described a pair of sandals with patterned beadwork. The thread holding the beads onto the sandals had rotted. The sandals looked fine, but as soon as someone tried to pick one up, it crumbled into a handful of beads. Even harsh lighting or humidity changes could damage items.

In the Antechamber, objects were stacked on top of each other and piled in heaps. Carter compared emptying the tomb to spillikins, a game similar

On one pair of Tutankhamen's sandals, the tops of the soles were decorated. Each sole featured a design of two bound captives, one from Nubia and one from Asia. These traditional enemies of Egypt were crushed every time Tut took a step.

to pick-up sticks, in which one item must be moved without disturbing any others. Just entering the Antechamber was a challenge because the Wishing Cup lay in the center of the doorway. Until the room was photographed and mapped, anyone entering the tomb was forced to carefully step over the cup.

CLEARING THE ANTECHAMBER

Carter and his team needed to clear the crowded Antechamber before the Burial Chamber could be officially opened. From December 27, 1922, to February 16, 1923, they worked to empty the Antechamber. Nearby tombs were used as a darkroom, a lunchroom, a lab, and a storeroom.

Carter worked slowly and meticulously to preserve the original tomb layout in his records. First he assigned each object a number. Photos were taken of the objects as they lay in each chamber. Carter made sure every object appeared in at least one photo and nothing was missed. The team mapped each object on the tomb floor, wrote a description of the object, and drew detailed sketches if needed. Items were conserved in the tomb if necessary and then moved to the conservation lab for repair. Large items, such as the animal couches, chariots, and shrines, had to be taken apart before they could be removed from the tomb. As each object was removed, it was carefully secured to a padded wooden stretcher.

One by one, each object was carefully removed from the tomb, including a shrine.

After conservation, each object was photographed again and then carefully packed for the trip to Cairo. To protect items in the Antechamber, Carter used 32 bales of calico fabric, more than one mile (1.6 km) of cotton padding, and huge quantities of surgical bandages.[7] Objects traveled on a hand-propelled railway, known as the Decauville railway, for 15 hours to the Nile River. From there they were shipped by boat to Cairo. Some extremely valuable objects, including the gold coffin and the funeral mask, were sent by train with an armed guard.

One artifact might also contain separate items that required cataloging and preservation. For example, the first artifact taken from the tomb was a chest called the Painted Box. This wooden chest was covered with painted plaster that depicted beautifully detailed hunting and battle scenes. Inside the Painted Box were many other objects—mostly clothing—in various stages of decay. One conservationist spent three weeks emptying this single box. The tomb had more than 50 boxes.

Sometimes articles that appeared to be in excellent condition inside the tomb decayed quickly

THE DECAUVILLE RAILWAY

Five and a half miles (8.9 km) of rough road lay between Carter's lab at the tomb and the river to Cairo. After artifacts were wrapped and put in cases, Carter had three options to get them to the river: camel, hand delivery, or the Decauville railway. Carter decided the railway was the least bumpy. The Decauville railway was a hand-propelled railway with no permanent track. Workmen moved the rails as they went. Objects were carefully packed into cases and loaded onto flat railcars. Once a railcar had traveled over a piece of track, the piece of railway was removed from the line, carried to the front of the line, and laid down again. Fifty workmen moved the rails forward in a continuous chain. It took 15 hours to go five and a half miles (8.9 km). Temperatures were often more than 100 degrees Fahrenheit (38°C), sometimes making the rails almost too hot to touch.

Carter's team had to work hard to protect the objects found in Tut's tomb, such as the Painted Box, from decay.

when they were moved to the air outside the tomb. The Painted Box, for example, seemed to be in good condition, but after three weeks in the conservation lab, the wood began shrinking. The painted plaster that covered the wood began buckling. To prevent further damage, Carter's team treated the box with melted paraffin wax. The wax acted like glue and held the plaster in place.

Carter's careful conservation preserved many objects that otherwise would have been destroyed and lost to history. Carter estimated that "without on-site conservation work, less than 1/10 of the artifacts would have survived to reach Cairo."[8] According to Carter, less than 0.25 percent of the tomb's objects were lost.

7

Problems Arise

The tomb was an overnight sensation, and Carter was suddenly famous. A string of dignitaries, officials, and other visitors—not to mention reporters—swarmed everywhere, interrupting Carter's work. Carter and Carnarvon officially opened the tomb on November 27, 1922. Two days later they held another opening ceremony, complete with a large formal dining table set up in the Valley of the Kings.

Visitors from across Egypt and around the world flocked to the Valley of the Kings to see Tut's tomb for themselves.

FINDING A PHOTOGRAPHER

When Carter first discovered the tomb, one of his most urgent needs was to find a photographer. The tomb had to be photographed before work could proceed. The Metropolitan Museum of Art in New York City had an Egyptian Expedition that was digging in Egypt. Carter asked if they could loan him a few people to help. The museum quickly agreed and sent Egyptologist Arthur Mace and photographer Harry Burton, who had worked with Theodore Davis during his excavation. Burton took hundreds of outstanding photographs. These photos provide a detailed record of the excavation and its artifacts.

From the start, Carter and Carnarvon faced the challenge of protecting the tomb from robbery. They had installed a heavy wooden gate after Lord Carnarvon's arrival, but they knew this would not be enough protection. As Carter noted, "The whole countryside was agog with excitement about the tomb; all sorts of extravagant tales were current about the gold and jewels it contained."[1] The last thing Carter wanted was a robbery, and a tomb full of priceless golden objects was a huge temptation.

PROTECTING THE TOMB

On December 3, 1922, Carter went to Cairo to order excavation supplies and a massive steel gate. Before Carter and Carnarvon left, they gave their workmen specific instructions to block the tomb door with wooden timbers and rebury the stairwell to protect the tomb. In fact, they would rebury the tomb every year in order to protect it until the next digging season. On December 17, a steel gate was installed in front of the tomb entrance. The keys to its four padlocks were carefully guarded by a member of Carter's team and were never out of sight. To protect against theft of small items, no one other than those on Carter's team were allowed to handle the tomb objects.

Three separate groups of guards, each working independently of one another, guarded the tomb. The Egyptian Antiquities Service provided one group of guards. The local authorities supplied another

A photograph by Harry Burton shows Egyptian workers removing a chariot wheel from Tut's tomb.

squad of soldiers. Carter also provided his own guard, made up of his most trusted workers.

Another difficulty for Carter was the challenge of keeping the artifacts in good condition. There were thousands of objects to record and preserve. The most important discovery in Egyptology was in Carter's care, and this responsibility weighed on him. Carter had gotten permission to use the tomb of Pharaoh Seti II as the location for his conservation lab. This tomb was located in a far corner of the Valley of the Kings and was rarely visited by tourists. The secluded tomb offered Carter's team privacy and plenty of room to work. The lab was also secure, thanks to a padlocked steel gate weighing 1.5 short tons (1.36 metric tons).[2] Carter insisted no visitors be allowed in the lab.

DISTRACTIONS

On December 22, work was again interrupted as Carter and Carnarvon hosted press and dignitaries. Carter estimated that during the first season, 25 percent of their time was spent giving tours to visitors. Every time someone famous came to visit, work on the tomb stopped while Carter and

Much to Carter's dismay, he and Carnarvon spent much of their time giving tours of the tomb, rather than excavating it.

Carnarvon played host. Even more troubling, visitors could, and often did, accidentally damage the tomb.

Hundreds of people, including friends, acquaintances, officials, and celebrities, wanted to see Tut's tomb. Outside the tomb, around the top of the stairwell, was a low wall. Every day crowds gathered along the wall, waiting to hear any news or perhaps see an artifact removed from the tomb. There were so many people, Carter worried the wall might collapse.

Telegrams and letters from around the world also swamped Carter. He received mail including everything from congratulations to souvenir requests to advice on how to calm evil spirits that might lurk in the tomb. The mail at the nearby post office doubled, then tripled, and the telegraph office was soon overrun with reporters.

WILD RUMORS

Carnarvon had decided to let only one newspaper officially cover the story. He chose the *Times*, a London newspaper. The *Times* would pay for the exclusive rights to the story. Carnarvon, in return, could recover some of his excavation costs and avoid dealing with hundreds of reporters.

It seemed like a good idea at the time, but Carnarvon's decision infuriated reporters from around the world, especially Egyptian reporters.

Tutankhamen's tomb was an enormously important discovery in their own country, and Egyptian reporters were not even able to report on it. Egyptians felt Carnarvon's actions were unfair. In the end, other newspapers had to print something, so they started printing rumors.

Soon wild stories began circulating about the tomb, including a rumor that three airplanes had landed in the Valley of the Kings, loaded up treasures, and flown off. Sometimes tomb workers gave out inaccurate information on purpose. Rumors spread like wildfire. Carter meanwhile felt hounded by paparazzi, saying, "Special correspondents at large salaries had [been] sent to interview us, report our every movement, and hide round corners to surprise a secret out of us."[3]

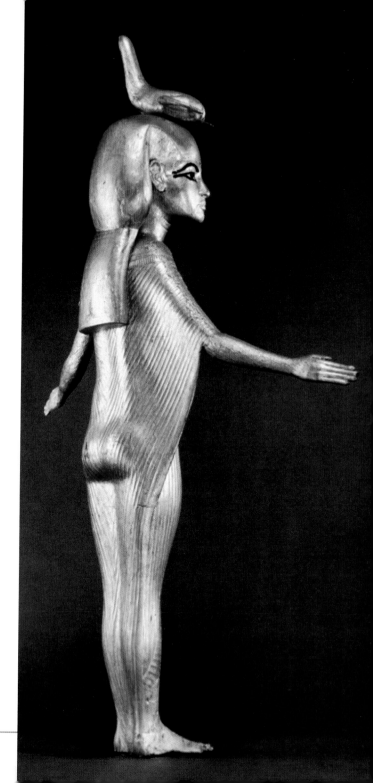

Tutankhamen's tomb was full of valuable treasure, such as this gilded statue.

TEMPERS FLARE

All these difficulties created a lot of stress. Emotions ran high. Nerves and tempers were frayed. Carter, who already had a reputation for being difficult and stubborn, became even more disagreeable. He snapped at the workmen, questioned the ability of other experts, and was irritable and cross.

Even Carter and Carnarvon, who had now been friends for many years, began arguing. There were many difficult decisions to be made, and they did not always agree. Most experts seem to think they differed regarding how to divide up the earnings from the tomb. Carnarvon was a collector and always wanted a generous share of the finds. But as an archaeologist, Carter thought the unique and priceless collection should not be broken up. At one point, the argument got so heated Carnarvon was banned from Carter's house.

On Friday, February 17, 1923, Carter and Carnarvon opened the Burial Chamber in front of an audience of approximately 20 people. They were grateful to discover thieves had not looted the royal burial. However, tensions still existed between Carter and Carnarvon, and everyone needed a break. On February 26, the team closed the tomb and then the lab. Carter returned to his house in Luxor. Carnarvon traveled to the south of Egypt.

THE DEATH OF LORD CARNARVON

While traveling, a mosquito bit Carnarvon. The bite became infected. Blood poisoning set in, then pneumonia, and on April 5, 1923, Lord Carnarvon died. He never got to see Tutankhamen's sarcophagus or mummy. Carter had lost his patron and friend. Carter continued working on the tomb after Carnarvon's death, but he faced one challenge after another. Problems may have plagued the excavation's first season, but the second season would be much worse.

THE MUMMY'S CURSE

Two weeks before Carnarvon died, the popular British author Marie Corelli predicted "dire punishment" would come to anyone who opened a sealed tomb.[4] After Carnarvon's death, some people began believing he had died because he opened Tut's tomb. He was a victim of the mummy's curse. People mistakenly attributed every bad event that happened to any excavation member as a sign of the curse. A cobra swallowed Carter's pet canary the day the tomb was opened. The lights in Cairo supposedly went out the moment Carnarvon died. Carnarvon's dog in Great Britain died the same day. These coincidences were said to be caused by the mummy's curse. However, infection in Egypt was common and so were cobras. Electricity in Cairo was always unreliable. Still, like other rumors, these stories gave newspaper reporters something to write about.

Clearing the Other Chambers

After the death of Lord Carnarvon, his wife, Lady Carnarvon, renewed his concession to the Valley of the Kings. The next digging season began in October 1923. Carter immediately began clearing the Burial Chamber. In February 1923, Carter and Carnarvon had first opened the Burial Chamber and seen a massive golden shrine. Now Carter was ready to examine it more closely. The gold shrine was similar to a giant box. It measured 17 feet (5.2 m) by 11 feet (3.4 m), and it stood 9 feet (2.7 m) tall.[1]

A wall painting on Tut's tomb shows King Ay, who took the throne after Tutankhamen, performing a ritual on Tut's mummy.

There was only a few feet of space between the shrine and the tomb walls. Apparently, the ancient Egyptian workmen who put together the shrine also had difficulty maneuvering in the small space because the shrine had not been put together correctly. The assembly directions written on the shrine in hieroglyphs had not been followed. The shrine was also facing east. According to Egyptian tradition, the shrine should face west, toward the setting sun and the Land of the Dead.

THE BURIAL CHAMBER

The double doors to the first shrine were closed and bolted but not sealed. Inside the first shrine was a sealed second shrine. Unlike the bolts on the first shrine, the bolts on the second shrine doors were sealed. Like the tomb doors, they bore the necropolis seal and Tutankhamen's seal. Above the second shrine stood a frame covered with a linen canopy, which was decorated with gilded bronze flowers. Inside the second shrine was a sealed third shrine. Inside the third shrine was a fourth, and inside the fourth shrine was the sarcophagus.

From October 1923 to February 1924, Carter worked to disassemble the four shrines. He then prepared to open the sarcophagus. The sarcophagus was a large stone coffin carved from quartzite. Its heavy lid was cracked in the middle, so Carter's team rigged a pulley system that would allow

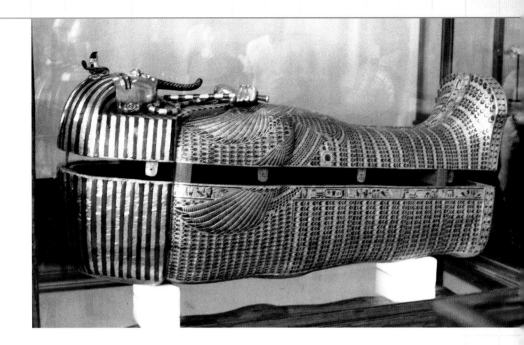

Tutankhamen's sarcophagus was filled with three separate coffins.

them to lift the lid without breaking it. On February 12, 1924, Carter and his team slowly raised the sarcophagus lid, which weighed more than one short ton (0.9 metric tons).[2] Inside the sarcophagus, wrapped in linen, lay a magnificent golden coffin. Carter later described the moment he first saw the gold coffin:

> *A gasp of wonderment escaped our lips, so gorgeous was the sight that met our eyes: a golden effigy of the young boy king, of the most magnificent workmanship.[3]*

MORE TROUBLE

The press was scheduled to tour the tomb the next day. A private tour for the archaeologists' wives and families was also scheduled. However, lingering bad feelings over the exclusion of Egyptians and the Egyptian press once again resurfaced. On the night of February 12, the Egyptian government sent Carter a telegram stating the press tour could proceed, but no family tour would be permitted. Carter and his team were outraged. A furious Carter issued a statement saying that because of "impossible restrictions and discourtesies . . . the tomb will be closed and no further work can be carried out."[4]

Carter left the sarcophagus lid suspended in the air and locked the tomb. He refused to give the keys to the Antiquities Service. The Antiquities Service responded by confiscating the tomb, cutting the locks, and canceling the concession. It would

TOMB PAINTINGS

The typical Egyptian tomb had walls painted with scenes of the afterlife. The paintings were done in vivid colors. Royal tombs were typically more detailed and elaborate. But in Tutankhamen's tomb, the Burial Chamber was the only painted room. The walls in Tutankhamen's burial chamber have a bright yellow background. The west wall of the Burial Chamber shows the journey of the sun through the Underworld and the 12 hours of night. Khepri, the god of the rising sun, is pictured as a scarab beetle. The east wall shows the funeral of Tutankhamen. The north wall shows Tutankhamen in the ceremony called the Opening of the Mouth and his welcome into the afterlife by the gods. The south wall is similar to the north—it shows the young pharaoh being welcomed by the gods.

The walls of Tutankhamen's burial chamber were painted with scenes and hieroglyphs.

take months of negotiation with Egyptian officials before Carter was allowed to resume work on the tomb. In the meantime, Carter left for Great Britain and then toured the United States giving lectures.

WORK RESUMES

Carter eventually returned to Egypt, and work resumed on January 25, 1925. There was little time left in the digging season, so Carter focused on conserving and documenting artifacts already in the lab. The tomb remained closed. The crowds and reporters soon left. It was a quiet but productive season. Carter shipped 19 cases of artifacts to Cairo and supervised their unpacking. As part of Carter's agreement with the Egyptian government, all objects found in the tomb were to remain in Egypt.

The next digging season began in early October 1925. Carter hoped to get as much work done as possible before tourists arrived. His goal was to remove Tutankhamen's mummy from the sarcophagus. This was much harder than expected. As with the shrines, the outer gold coffin was the first coffin of several. The coffin had a humanlike shape, and it was built like a Russian nesting doll. Two more coffins lay inside the first coffin, each tightly fitted inside the other. In fact, they were so tight, Carter could not even squeeze his little finger in between the two coffins. Both coffins were made from wood overlaid with gold foil, but the second coffin was more ornate. It had inlays made from glass, faience, and semiprecious stones. The condition of the second coffin was not as good as the first coffin, and it appeared to have some moisture damage. Inside the second coffin was a third coffin. This coffin was made of solid gold. Unfortunately, it was also covered with a tarry black substance that caused the two coffins to stick together. In ancient times, ointment had been poured over the coffin as part of the burial. Eventually the ointment had hardened and cemented the coffins together.

THE MUMMY REVEALED

After removing the lid of the third coffin, Carter finally beheld the mummy of Tutankhamen, which he described as an "impressive, neat, and carefully made mummy."[5] The mummy was wrapped in linen, which was fastened with inscribed bands made of gold. Golden hands sewn onto the linen held the royal crook and flail, two symbols of ancient Egyptian pharaohs. Except for its head and feet, the mummy was covered in the same black resin as the third coffin. A stunning golden mask was placed over the mummy's head.

Carter and his team prepared to remove the mummy from the coffin. The hardened resins had glued the mummy to the inner coffin. The team tried placing the mummy out in the sun, hoping the heat would soften the resin. When that failed, they decided to examine the mummy in the coffin. Before they began, they covered the decayed linen wrappings with melted paraffin wax to help hold the wrappings together.

AMULETS

Magic amulets were placed in mummy wrappings as protection. The Egyptian word for amulet is *meket*, which means "protector." Egyptians often wore them around their necks. Amulets were made from semiprecious stones, metal, wood, bone, and faience. Egyptians believed an amulet made from the wrong material would not work. Two common amulets were the wedjat eye and the scarab beetle.

DIGGING
DEEPER

Unwrapping a Mummy

The first examination of Tutankhamen's mummy was on November 11, 1925. Dr. Douglas Derry sliced through 16 layers of bandages to get to the body. Because resin stuck the mummy to the coffin, Derry had to break apart the body to get it out of the coffin. He separated the body at the head, shoulders, elbows, hands, hips, knees, and ankles. He cut the torso in half. He extracted the head from the gold mask by inserting hot knives to break apart the resin.

Derry's examination of the wisdom teeth and bone growth plates indicated Tutankhamen died between the ages of 17 and 19. The mummy also had a ragged embalming cut that was unusually large—it stretched all the way from his belly button to his hipbone. Because Tut died so young, Carter and his team wondered how he had died. But Derry's autopsy did little to unravel this mystery. More recent examinations of Tutankhamen's mummy have provided clues to how the young pharaoh may have died.

On November 11, Dr. Douglas Derry, a professor of anatomy, began an autopsy of Tutankhamen. First he made a long lengthwise slit through the wrappings. He and Carter had hoped only the outer wrappings would be glued to the coffin, but the inner wrappings were just as firmly stuck. Derry carefully peeled back the wrappings and uncovered jewelry and sacred amulets placed throughout the wrappings. Carter counted 143 objects on the mummy, including everything from bracelets to daggers to the golden finger and toe sheaths, which fit over Tut's individually wrapped fingers and toes.[6]

After unwrapping the mummy, Derry tried chiseling it out of the coffin. He also tried cutting it out with heated knives. When these failed, he cut the mummy in half and removed it in sections. At the time, most Egyptologists were more interested in the objects buried with mummies than the mummies themselves. People did not fully realize the valuable information mummies contained. Derry's handling greatly damaged the mummy, and today much greater care would have been taken.

THE TREASURY

On December 31, the solid gold coffin and mummy mask traveled to Cairo under armed guard. Carter and his team spent the rest of the season conserving the coffins and jewelry. There were still two rooms to be excavated, the room beyond the Burial Chamber, known as the Treasury, and the small room off the Antechamber, known as the Annex. The rooms had been examined years earlier, but they had been mostly ignored while the excavators focused on the Antechamber and Burial Room. The Treasury remained boarded up until Carter's team was finally ready to begin its excavation in October 1926.

When Carter had examined the Treasury originally in 1923, he saw thieves had disturbed a few boxes, but most of the boxes still had intact seals. The Treasury held more than 500 objects.[7] One of the most important objects in the Treasury was a gilded shrine that contained Tutankhamen's canopic jars. The lids to Tutankhamen's canopic jars were shaped like his head.

Another important discovery was two small caskets, each holding a mummified unborn child. These two premature fetuses were female. One died at approximately five months into the pregnancy, and the other at approximately two months before birth. Egyptologists believe these are the daughters of Tutankhamen and his wife, Ankhesenamen.

PRESERVING ORGANS IN CANOPIC JARS

When a person was mummified, embalmers removed the internal organs through a small slit in the left side of the body. The heart was left in the body. Egyptians believed humans thought with their heart. The deceased would need the heart to think as well as for a weighing of the heart ceremony, which was thought to determine whether or not a person could enter the afterlife. Four canopic jars held internal organs: the liver, lungs, stomach, and intestines. Embalming fluid was poured into each jar to preserve the organs.

Canopic jars held Tut's organs.

THE ANNEX

The Annex was the last room Carter excavated, and it was a huge challenge. Tomb robbers had ransacked the room, and objects were strewn everywhere. Although it was the smallest room in the tomb, the Annex held more than 2,000 individual items.[8] Because the entire floor was covered, excavators had to remove objects while suspended on ropes, as if they were spiders dangling from a thread, until there was enough floor space to stand on. Clearing the Annex took from November 1927 until spring 1928.

Year after year, the conservation work continued. On November 10, 1930, the last artifact was removed from the tomb. In February 1932, the last shipment of objects was sent to Cairo.

Carter spent almost ten years excavating Tutankhamen's tomb. He had pages and pages of notes, photographs, maps, descriptions, and even three introductory books about the excavation. For several years he wanted to write a thorough, six-volume scientific study about the tomb, but he made little progress and eventually gave up. Carter died on March 2, 1939. Shortly after Carter's death, his complete records were donated to the Griffith Institute, an Egyptology research center at Oxford University in Great Britain. The definitive, full, and complete study of Tutankhamen's tomb has yet to be written.

Tut Today

Tutankhamen is the only pharaoh found undisturbed in an intact tomb. The Egyptian Antiquities Service thought he should stay there, so they decided to return the mummy to the tomb rather than send it to the Cairo Museum. After Derry's examination, the body was reassembled on a tray filled with sand and photographed. The mummy and the sand-filled tray were both put into the largest outer coffin and then lowered into the sarcophagus. He did not lay untouched, however. Since Derry's autopsy, a

Egyptologist Zahi Hawass's 2007 examination of Tutankhamen's mummy revealed surprising new information.

number of experts have examined Tutankhamen. As science and technology improved, new techniques were used to study Tutankhamen's mummy, his artifacts, and his tomb.

THE 1968 AND 1978 X-RAYS

After Carter and Derry's autopsy of Tut in 1925, Tut's mummy was not studied again until the 1960s. In 1968, Liverpool University anatomy professor Ronald Harrison opened the sarcophagus for another examination of Tut. He found Tut's body unwrapped and lying on the sand tray. Today researchers do not usually unwrap mummies. Instead experts use less damaging techniques, such as 3-D X-rays and tissue samples. Harrison's team was not allowed to remove Tut from his tomb, but they took a skin sample and used a portable X-ray scanner to examine the mummy. The skin sample showed Tutankhamen was related to some of the mummies found in the Valley of the Kings tomb KV55.

In addition to observing the resin in the mummy's skull, Harrison also noticed a small piece of bone in the skull. Harrison said it appeared this bone fragment was caused after death. Later, experts realized there were actually two bone fragments. The bone fragments have led some experts to think a blow to the back of his head may have killed Tut.

In 1925, Derry had not fully examined the upper torso because of the resin-soaked linen that packed the chest. In 1968, however, Harrison discovered obvious damage to the chest. The breastbone, heart, and some ribs were missing. Harrison did not think Derry had caused this damage during his examination. Harrison believed it had been done at or before the time the body was mummified.

FROM LOW TECH TO HIGH TECH

The archaeological procedures Carter used seem primitive by today's standards, but he tried to use the best techniques available at the time. Today, technological advances have created unusual new methods for studying ancient civilizations. One new technique archaeologists are using is satellites. Just as CT scans allow doctors to see inside the body, satellite images often reveal features in the landscape that cannot easily be seen with the naked eye. One archaeologist, Sarah Parcak, uses infrared satellite pictures to detect items such as bricks buried underground. Working in Egypt, her team has found 17 possible pyramids, 3,000 settlements, and 1,000 tombs.[1]

In 1978, James Harris, an orthodontics professor from the University of Michigan, also X-rayed Tutankhamen. His exam focused on Tut's head and teeth. Harris found similarities between the head of Tut and the head of KV55 mummies. These similarities are significant because most

Egyptologists believe the mummies in KV55 are from the Amarna Period. Many Egyptologists believe the head similarities suggest KV55 contained the mummy of Tut's father Akhenaton.

THE 2005 EXAMINATION

Tut's mummy was not examined again until 2005. Dr. Zahi Hawass of the Egyptian Supreme Council of Antiquities analyzed the mummy using modern scientific techniques. Hawass and his team did DNA testing. They used CT scans to create a 3-D image of the mummy. They reached several new conclusions based on the CT scans and DNA evidence. They confirmed Tut's chest was damaged, probably before mummification. They also concluded the bone fragments were caused either during embalming or during Derry's autopsy, after Tut's death. They found Tut's pelvic bones were almost totally missing. His left thigh had been broken at, or near, the time of death. They also uncovered evidence Tut may have had other health problems, including a clubfoot, cleft palate, scoliosis, and malaria. Not all researchers agree with the team's conclusions.

In February 2010, a team of scientists released the results from the 2005 DNA tests done on Tutankhamen and other royal mummies in the Egyptian Museum. The scientists were looking for family connections between the mummies. Ancient DNA is very hard to extract, and it is often contaminated,

Testing on the mummified body of Queen Tiy has suggested she may be Tutankhamen's grandmother.

but the scientific team reached a number of conclusions about Tut's relatives. They determined Akhenaton was in fact Tutankhamen's father. A mummy found in KV55 is Tutankhamen's mother. Another KV55 mummy is his grandmother Queen Tiy. In spite of the evidence of malaria, experts do not agree whether malaria was the actual cause of his death or not. Because of the questionable DNA, not all scientists agree with the team's findings.

No one knows for sure how Tutankhamen died. There are many different theories. Some think he was murdered. Others think perhaps he got an infection after breaking his leg. Some think he might have died of malaria. Others have wondered if he had a genetic disease. Perhaps he had an accident while hunting or battling foreign enemies. Dr. W. Benson Harer Jr., an amateur Egyptologist, thinks a hippopotamus killed Tutankhamen. Some researchers are using computer simulations to study whether Tut may have been killed by a chariot running over him. Despite many theories, the cause of Tut's death remains a mystery to this day.

In 2007, after Hawass's study, the mummy was moved to a glass coffin with special temperature and humidity controls. The coffin was returned to Tut's tomb. Today the boy king lies where he was buried, in his sarcophagus in his tomb in the Valley of the Kings. Every year, thousands journey to see his tomb. Millions of people also visit Tutankhamen's treasures, which are on display at the Egyptian Museum in Cairo.

MASK MYSTERY

Today, many artifacts from Tut's tomb are on display at the Egyptian Museum in Cairo. Some artifacts are in storage. Many are in other Egyptian museums. A few of Tut's artifacts found their way out of Egypt, likely taken by Carnarvon for his private collection. Carter identified 5,398 objects in the tomb, and many need more study.

Surprisingly, Tut's golden mask, which is one of the most famous Egyptian objects in history, was not seriously studied since the 1920s. But in 2010, Egyptologist Nicholas Reeves presented new research on the mask. According to Reeves, the famous golden mask of Tutankhamen was not intended for Tut at all. Reeves thinks the mask's face, which looks like Tut, was made and then attached to a headdress originally created for someone else.

Reeves said a number of clues led him to this conclusion. The mask is made of separate face and headdress pieces, and there are rivets and soldering lines around the face and neck. Reeves also points out that the mask and the headdress are not made from the same materials. The face is made from bluish-silvery gold, while the headdress is made from more yellowish gold. The blue materials on the headdress and face do not

Reeves believes Tutankhamen's gold funerary mask may have actually been made for someone else.

تابوت الذهب الخالص للملك توت عنخ آمون كان يغطي رأس وأكتاف مومياء الملك
يبلغ وزن جزء عظيم للغاية للملك على يمكن أرتداؤه على مومياء الملك حتى تتم حمايتها
القناع جميع صفات المصري القديمة   والقناع يمثل الملك مرتدي غطاء الرأس القماشي
الملكي المخطط رأس العمر، والوجه الحقيقية المستعارة ويغطيه من خلفه شعر بكثافة

match either. The blue on the headdress is made from glass, while the blue on the face is faience. If the mask and headdress had been made at the same time, they would probably be made from the same materials.

Reeves also thinks the earring holes prove the mask was originally for a female. Women and children in Egypt wore earrings, but boys usually stopped wearing earrings once they reached adolescence. The earring holes punched through the mask are covered with small gold discs, and Reeves thinks these small gold plugs were added to make the mask more masculine for Tut.

Other evidence from Tut's tomb supports Reeves's theory. Researchers believe Tut was buried in a small tomb probably intended for a nobleman and that his funeral was rushed. Straps found on Tut's mummy show the cartouche of Neferneferuaten. This is the name of Nefertiti, one of the wives of Pharaoh Akhenaton. Other objects found in the tomb bear traces of Nefertiti's cartouche or were clearly made for someone other than Tut.

TUT'S CHARIOTS

The chariots found in Tut's tomb have also been studied. Six complete chariots were found dismantled in Tut's tomb. Before Carter discovered Tut's tomb, only two complete Egyptian chariots were known to exist. In 2001,

Bela Sandor, professor of engineering at the University of Wisconsin, began studying Tut's chariots at the Egyptian Museum in Cairo.

According to Sandor, Tut's chariots represent "the earliest high performance machine."[2] Chariots were not invented in Egypt, but Egyptians refined chariot design. They added parts that worked like springs and shock absorbers. They included parts that helped prevent rollovers. They moved the axle from the center of the chariot to the back, which helped make the ride less bumpy. In 2013, a team of archaeologists, engineers, woodworkers, and horse trainers built two replicas of Egyptian chariots and tested them to study how Egyptian chariots work.

PRESERVING THE TOMB

Important efforts are being made to preserve Tut's tomb, one of the most popular sites in the Valley of the Kings.

ANOTHER TOMB MORE SPECTACULAR THAN TUT'S?

Some of the objects in Tut's tomb bear the cartouche of Nefertiti, wife of Akhenaton. Reeves has proposed a controversial theory that perhaps Nefertiti ruled, and died, as pharaoh. Some of the objects buried with Nefertiti as pharaoh were then used later in Tut's tomb. Reeves also believes there may be one more intact tomb in the Valley of the Kings—Nefertiti's. If found, Reeves thinks this tomb would be even more spectacular than Tut's.

Egyptian authorities worry the volume of visitors is damaging the tomb. Even small changes in temperature and humidity are a concern. The Getty Conservation Institute (GCI) is an art conservation organization working to preserve Tut's tomb. In 2009, the GCI began studying Tut's tomb and recording its condition. It tried to find the causes of the tomb's deterioration. In 2011, GCI researchers began testing and evaluating ways to conserve the tomb. As a result, features to better preserve the tomb were put in place. Tomb walkways, barriers, ventilation, lights, and signs were updated.

In an effort to limit visitors and preserve Tut's tomb, a replica of Tut's tomb was built in Luxor near the home of Howard Carter. Egyptian antiquities experts hope the exact replica lets visitors experience Tut's tomb yet preserve the original tomb. The company that designed and built the replica, Factum Arte, measured 100 million points for every square meter in the tomb and used laser scanners to match the tomb's exact colors, shapes, and textures. Tut's real tomb can only be visited by limited numbers of people for short periods of time, but the replica allows more people to stay longer.

TUT'S LEGACY

Tut reigned during the Eighteenth Dynasty, one of the wealthiest periods in Egypt's history. His intact tomb was the most complete royal treasure ever discovered. His tomb reveals not only the spectacular wealth of Egypt but also objects of religious and ceremonial importance, as well as objects that provide clues about what everyday life was like in ancient Egypt. The artifacts in Tutankhamen's tomb uncovered new and important information about Egyptian art, culture, and the history of the New Kingdom. The tomb introduced millions of people to ancient Egypt. It also increased general interest in archaeology.

More than 3,000 years have passed since Tutankhamen reigned as pharaoh of Egypt. Yet he continues to influence and intrigue people around the world. Tutankhamen and his name live on.

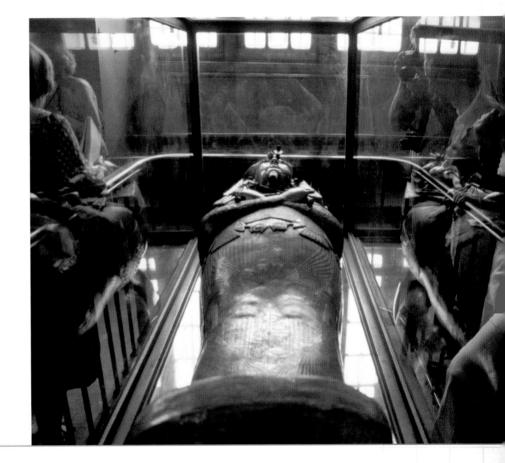

Visitors can view one of Tut's golden coffins at the Egyptian Museum in Cairo.

TIMELINE

1333–1323 BCE

Tutankhamen reigns as pharaoh.

1891 CE

Archaeologist William Matthew Flinders Petrie finds objects bearing Tut's name during an excavation at Amarna.

1905–1909

Theodore Davis excavates in the Valley of the Kings and finds more evidence of Tutankhamen.

JUNE 1914

Lord Carnarvon and Howard Carter receive the concession to excavate in the Valley of the Kings.

FALL 1917

Carnarvon and Carter begin their excavation at the Valley of the Kings.

NOVEMBER 4, 1922

Carter discovers the first step leading to Tutankhamen's tomb.

NOVEMBER 27, 1922

Tut's tomb is officially opened.

APRIL 5, 1923

Lord Carnarvon dies of an infected mosquito bite.

NOVEMBER 11, 1925

Dr. Douglas Derry begins his autopsy of Tut.

NOVEMBER 10, 1930

The final objects are removed from the tomb.

MARCH 2, 1939

Howard Carter dies.

2005

Dr. Zahi Hawass performs DNA testing on Tut, confirming he is Akhenaton's son and that two mummies in KV55 are his mother and grandmother.

DIGGING UP THE FACTS

DATE OF DISCOVERY

Howard Carter discovered King Tut's tomb in the Valley of the Kings in Egypt on November 4, 1922.

KEY PLAYERS

- Howard Carter was the chief archaeologist who led the excavation of Tutankhamen's tomb.

- George Herbert, fifth Earl of Carnarvon, was the wealthy amateur Egyptologist who funded the excavation.

- Dr. Douglas Derry was a professor of anatomy who performed an autopsy on Tut's mummy in 1925.

- Dr. Zahi Hawass is the Egyptian archaeologist who led DNA testing on Tut's mummy in 2005.

KEY TECHNOLOGIES

Carter and Carnarvon's original excavation relied on manual labor, photography, scale drawings, basic engineering, and cleaning solvents. As more technologies became available, new tools were used. Modern archaeologists, such as Hawass, used DNA testing and CT scanning to study Tut's mummy.

IMPACT ON SCIENCE

The discovery of Tut's tomb revealed new information about the prosperous New Kingdom era. It showed archaeologists how a pharaoh was buried, and it also increased interest in archaeology and Egyptology around the world. The discovery of Tutankhamen helped uncover identities of other mummies in the Valley of the Kings.

SEEING TUT'S TREASURES

Since the 1960s, artifacts recovered from Tutankhamen's tomb have gone on a number of world tours, making the boy king more famous than ever. The artifacts' permanent home is at the Egyptian Museum in Cairo. This is the best place to see Tut's treasures in person. In the past, thousands of tourists have made the trip to the Valley of the Kings to see Tut's tomb. However the flood of visitors has greatly damaged the tomb. So, officials built an exact replica of the tomb in Luxor, Egypt. Officials hope this replica will help protect the original from further damage.

QUOTE

"At first I could see nothing, the hot air escaping from the chamber causing the candle flame to flicker, but presently, as my eyes grew accustomed to the light, details of the room within emerged slowly from the mist, strange animals, statues, and gold—everywhere the glint of gold . . . . When Lord Carnarvon, unable to stand the suspense any longer, inquired anxiously, 'Can you see anything?' It was all I could do to get out the words, 'Yes, wonderful things.'"—*Howard Carter*

GLOSSARY

amulet
A magical charm worn for protection.

antiquity
An artifact from ancient times.

autopsy
A medical examination of a corpse.

cache
A collection of mummies placed together in a tomb.

cartouche
An oval ring surrounding a royal Egyptian's name.

draftsman
An artist hired to draw plans and sketches of buildings and artifacts at excavation sites.

dynasty
A line of related rulers of a country.

Egyptology
The study of ancient Egypt.

embalming
The act of preserving a dead body.

hieroglyph
Ancient Egyptian writing in which certain pictures represent words or phrases.

meticulous
Extremely careful and detail oriented.

protectorate
A small country that is controlled and protected by a larger one.

sarcophagus
A coffin made of stone.

shrine
A building or shelter that holds something considered sacred.

ADDITIONAL RESOURCES

SELECTED BIBLIOGRAPHY

Allen, Susan J. *Tutankhamen's Tomb: The Thrill of Discovery.* New York: Metropolitan Museum of Art, 2006. Print.

Carter, Howard, and A. C. Mace. *The Tomb of Tut.Ankh.Amen.* Vol. 1. London: Cassell, 1923. Reprint. Foreword by Nicholas Reeves. London: Gerald Duckworth, 2003. Print.

FURTHER READINGS

MacDonald, Angela. *Write Your Own Egyptian Hieroglyphs.* Berkeley, CA: U of California P, 2007. Print.

Napoli, Donna Jo. *Treasury of Egyptian Mythology: Classic Stories of Gods, Goddesses, Monsters & Mortals.* Washington, DC: National Geographic, 2013. Print.

Putnam, James. *Mummy.* New York: DK, 2009. Print.

WEBSITES

To learn more about Digging Up the Past, visit **booklinks.abdopublishing.com**. These links are routinely monitored and updated to provide the most current information available.

FOR MORE INFORMATION

For more information on this subject, contact or visit the following organizations:

THE GRIFFITH INSTITUTE
Sackler Library
1 Saint John Street
Oxford, England OX1 2LG
+44 (0) 1865 278097
http://www.griffith.ox.ac.uk
The Griffith Institute is an Egyptology research institute established in 1939. Located at the University of Oxford in England, the Griffith Institute's collection *Tutankhamen: Anatomy of an Excavation* covers Howard Carter and Lord Carnarvon's discovery of Tutankhamen's tomb.

THE ORIENTAL INSTITUTE OF THE UNIVERSITY OF CHICAGO
1155 East Fifty-Eighth Street
Chicago, IL 60637
773-702-9514
http://oi.uchicago.edu
This research organization and museum is committed to studying ancient civilizations of the Middle East. Its museum collection includes an enormous statue of Tutankhamen and other artifacts from ancient Egypt.

SOURCE NOTES

Chapter 1. The Fascinating Pharaoh

1. Howard Carter and A. C. Mace. *The Tomb of Tut.Ankh.Amen.* Vol. 1. London: Cassell, 1923. Reprint. Foreword by Nicholas Reeves. London: Gerald Duckworth, 2003. Print. 96.
2. Ibid.
3. Ibid.
4. Nicholas Reeves and John H. Taylor. *Howard Carter before Tutankhamen.* New York: Abrams, 1993. Print. 155.

Chapter 2. Tutankhamen's Life and Reign

None.

Chapter 3. Clues to Tutankhamen

1. Bob Brier. *The Murder of Tutankhamen.* New York: G. P. Putnam's Sons, 1998. Print. 135.
2. Nicholas Reeves. *The Complete Tutankhamun: The King, The Tomb, The Royal Treasure.* London: Thames and Hudson, 1990. Print. 36.
3. Howard Carter and A. C. Mace. *The Tomb of Tut.Ankh.Amen.* Vol. 1. London: Cassell, 1923. Reprint. Foreword by Nicholas Reeves. London: Gerald Duckworth, 2003. Print. 78.
4. Ibid.

Chapter 4. Finding the Tomb

1. Howard Carter and A. C. Mace. *The Tomb of Tut.Ankh.Amen.* Vol. 1. London: Cassell, 1923. Reprint. Foreword by Nicholas Reeves. London: Gerald Duckworth, 2003. Print. 82.
2. T. G. H. James. *Howard Carter: The Path to Tutankhamun.* London: Kegan Paul, 2001. Print. 215.
3. Howard Carter and A. C. Mace. *The Tomb of Tut.Ankh.Amen.* Vol. 1. London: Cassell, 1923. Reprint. Foreword by Nicholas Reeves. London: Gerald Duckworth, 2003. Print. xxviii.
4. Ibid. 94.
5. Ibid. 84–85.
6. Ibid. 86.
7. Ibid. 85.
8. Nicholas Reeves and John H. Taylor. *Howard Carter before Tutankhamun.* New York: Abrams, 1993. Print. 40.
9. Howard Carter and A. C. Mace. *The Tomb of Tut.Ankh.Amen.* Vol. 1. London: Cassell, 1923. Reprint. Foreword by Nicholas Reeves. London: Gerald Duckworth, 2003. Print. 88.

Chapter 5. Opening the Tomb

1. Howard Carter and A. C. Mace. *The Tomb of Tut.Ankh.Amen.* Vol. 1. London: Cassell, 1923. Reprint. Foreword by Nicholas Reeves. London: Gerald Duckworth, 2003. Print. 89–90.

2. Ibid. 90.

3. Ibid. 91.

4. Nicholas Reeves and John H. Taylor. *Howard Carter before Tutankhamun.* New York: Abrams, 1993. Print. 66.

5. Ibid. 66–67.

6. Howard Carter and A. C. Mace. *The Tomb of Tut.Ankh.Amen.* Vol. 1. London: Cassell, 1923. Reprint. Foreword by Nicholas Reeves. London: Gerald Duckworth, 2003. Print. 88, 94.

7. Joyce Tyldesley. *Tutankhamen: The Search for an Egyptian King.* New York: Basic, 2012. Print. 60.

8. Howard Carter and A. C. Mace. *The Tomb of Tut.Ankh.Amen.* Vol. 1. London: Cassell, 1923. Reprint. Foreword by Nicholas Reeves. London: Gerald Duckworth, 2003. Print. 94.

9. Ibid. 95–96.

Chapter 6. Inside the Tomb

1. Nicholas Reeves. *The Complete Tutankhamun: The King, The Tomb, The Royal Treasure.* London: Thames and Hudson, 1990. Print. 79.

2. Bob Brier. *The Murder of Tutankhamen.* New York: G. P. Putnam's Sons, 1998. Print. 144.

3. Ibid. 145.

4. Joyce Tyldesley. *Tutankhamen: The Search for an Egyptian King.* New York: Basic, 2012. Print. 118.

5. Kate Santon. *Tutankhamun: The Treasures of the Golden King.* Bath, UK: Parragon, 2007. Print. 55.

6. Ibid.

7. Howard Carter and A. C. Mace. *The Tomb of Tut.Ankh.Amen.* Vol. 1. London: Cassell, 1923. Reprint. Foreword by Nicholas Reeves. London: Gerald Duckworth, 2003. Print. 107.

8. Joyce Tyldesley. *Tutankhamen: The Search for an Egyptian King.* New York: Basic, 2012. Print. 107.

Chapter 7. Problems Arise

1. Howard Carter and A. C. Mace. *The Tomb of Tut.Ankh.Amen.* Vol. 1. London: Cassell, 1923. Reprint. Foreword by Nicholas Reeves. London: Gerald Duckworth, 2003. Print. 100.

2. Ibid. 129.

3. Ibid. 141.

4. Nicholas Reeves and John H. Taylor. *Howard Carter before Tutankhamun.* New York: Abrams, 1993. Print. 157.

Chapter 8. Clearing the Other Chambers

1. Howard Carter and A. C. Mace. *The Tomb of Tut.Ankh.Amen.* Vol. 1. London: Cassell, 1923. Reprint. Foreword by Nicholas Reeves. London: Gerald Duckworth, 2003. Print. 182.

2. Nicholas Reeves. *The Complete Tutankhamun: The King, The Tomb, The Royal Treasure.* London: Thames and Hudson, 1990. Print. 105.

3. Howard Carter and A. C. Mace. *The Tomb of Tut.Ankh.Amen.* Vol. 1. London: Cassell, 1923. Reprint. Foreword by Nicholas Reeves. London: Gerald Duckworth, 2003. Print. 51–52.

4. Joyce Tyldesley. *Tutankhamen: The Search for an Egyptian King.* New York: Basic, 2012. Print. 92.

5. Howard Carter and A. C. Mace. *The Tomb of Tut.Ankh.Amen.* Vol. 1. London: Cassell, 1923. Reprint. Foreword by Nicholas Reeves. London: Gerald Duckworth, 2003. Print. 82–83.

6. Ibid. 137.

7. Nicholas Reeves. *The Complete Tutankhamun: The King, The Tomb, The Royal Treasure.* London: Thames and Hudson, 1990. Print. 88.

8. Ibid. 89.

Chapter 9. Tut Today

1. Hannah Bloch. "Satellite Archaeology." *National Geographic* 223.2 (February 2013): 60. Print.

2. Bela I. Sandor. "The Rise and Decline of the Tutankhamun-class Chariot." *Oxford Journal of Archaeology.* 23.2. (2 June 2004): 153. Print.

INDEX

ABOUT THE AUTHOR

Shannon Baker Moore is a freelance writer and editor who writes for both adults and children. A college writing instructor and writing coach, she is a member of the Society of Children's Book Writers & Illustrators and the Missouri Writers' Guild. Author of *The Korean War* for Abdo's Essential Library of American Wars series, Shannon also blogs about children's books. She and her family have lived throughout the United States, but they currently call Saint Louis, Missouri, home.